MW01236260

UNDERGROUND FOOTBALL
LEGENDS
AND THE IMPORTANCE OF EDUCATION

DIFFERENCE BETWEEN A DREAM AND FANTASY

UNDERGROUND FOOTBALL
LEGENDS
AND THE IMPORTANCE OF EDUCATION

DEON LAMAR COAST

TATE PUBLISHING
AND ENTERPRISES, LLC

Published by Tate Publishing & Enterprises, LLC
127 E. Trade Center Terrace | Mustang, Oklahoma 73064 USA
1.888.361.9473 | www.tatepublishing.com

Tate Publishing is committed to excellence in the publishing industry. The company reflects the philosophy established by the founders, based on Psalm 68:11,
"The Lord gave the word and great was the company of those who published it."

Published in the United States of America

ISBN: 978-1-63306-523-9
Biography & Autobiography / Sports
15.02.06

I dedicate this book to my grandparents, William and Victoria Kennedy and Joe Lee and Lenora Coast. I was blessed to have met them all, may their souls rest in peace. I also dedicate this book to every young athlete and all dream chasers across the world reaching their full potential but never neglecting education, for it is the best tool to reaching for success and living a good life without taking useless risks. Reach for the heavens and you shall get beyond the stars. I also dedicate this book to my mother, Kate M. Kennedy, for never giving up on me and my dreams; if it was not for her, where would I be. Thank God for giving me the mother that I was blessed with because nobody else could have endured the struggles with me. I dedicate this book to my cousins Jonathan Brown, III, Wesley Kennedy, III and Eric Brown, my nephews Jamell Coast, Jr., Jalil Coast and my son Jaden Coast I asked them all one by one what they wanted to be when they graduate from college, the only one with a profession in mind was, my cousin Jonathan Brown II. They all play sports, but by the time this book is published, I hope that they will take their education more seriously.

Contents

Introduction

I want to start this true story by saying that everything happens for a reason and fate has no exceptions. If you find that your dreams turn out to be a nightmare, this story is definitely for you. This story is to inspire every young athlete, boy or girl with extraordinary talent, and those with the determination at heart who never quits informing them of how important it is getting your education and realizing that destiny can have different intentions for us all and no love for our dreams. Life can sometimes snatch our innermost desires, this is one of the greatest stories you will ever hear about a family of football players who was less fortunate of actually achieving the professional level and never took seriously the importance of education. My name is Deon Lamar Coast. I was born on 1983 in Savannah, Georgia. My mother is Kate

Marie Kennedy and she raised my brother, Jamell Coast, and I alone. This story kicks off when she married my father, Nathaniel Coast.

My father did not raise my brother and me; we hardly saw him our whole life. Everything that I learned about football, I owe to my two uncles, Wesley Kennedy Sr. and Anthony Kennedy. My uncle, Wesley Kennedy, is now a minister at Second St. Luke Baptist Church in Savannah, Georgia. Though he was a baseball star, he kicked the first high school field goal in Savannah, Georgia. My uncle, Anthony Kennedy, the youngest male of eight siblings, died from terminal cancer as a result of abusing drugs at the age of forty-two. My father, who was one of the greatest football players to ever live, attended Tompkins High School. It was turned to a middle school and then back to a high school, he was known as Coast, The Work Horse number 44.

He was coached by the great Joe Turner. My father was a defensive player when he began playing football, from which most great offensive players' first position starts. It was by fate, he became a running back. One game they put him in the back field as a blocker for punting special teams. When the ball was snapped, it became a fumble. My father picked it up and ran a seventy-five yard touchdown. This was the true birth of Coast, The Work Horse. Throughout his high school career, he achieved the title as the best running back that Tompkins High School had ever seen. During his senior year in 1968, he ran for over 1,300 yards and twenty–four touchdowns. He was Florida A & M University first round pick and started running back until he had a knee injury, but they still started him at flanker. This took a shot at the Work Horse's ego, it made him angry and his reckless behavior started to get the best of him. During my father's senior year at Florida A & M, the Chicago Bears and the Huston Oilers sent him letters to be drafted to the NFL. I feel like to this day, if it was not for a knee injury and a very wild night before free agent camp where the draft is to begin, my father would have easily played professional football. The night before camp, my father and three teammates were involved in a robbery attempt that could have landed him and his teammates in jail. As a result, he was shot on the hand. Somehow there was suspicion that these criminals belong to Florida A & M football team. My father was the only one with evidence of a gunshot wound in his hand and started back home to Savannah Georgia. His football career came to an end along with his chance to graduate from college.

Anthony Kennedy known as Breeze was much younger than my father, but attended the same Tompkins High School. After his high school career, he wanted to attend Savannah State because of the love for a female. Savannah state turned him down but California State welcomed him. When he got there, they had his named posted on highway billboards, and it read "California State welcomes Anthony Kennedy." After signing with California State, he then became homesick and desperately wanted to move back home. He then signed a contract with Albany State. This would give him the chance to take revenge on the school of his first choice, Savannah State, which they played against. My uncle, Anthony Kennedy, punished the tigers by scoring four touchdowns for turning him down on his application. It was drugs and women that got the best of my uncle, which was usually the downfall of most of the men in my family. Most notably, their lack of focus on their education was detrimental. While at Albany State, he finished his football career in college, but he did not graduate in his class. The love of his life was pregnant from another man; he loved her so much, he was willing to take the responsibility for the baby even though there was no way that it could be his child. My uncle then turned to drugs, which not only changed his life, but ultimately took his life, leaving behind his wife, Georgia Blige Kennedy, and two track-and-field star daughters, ShaNika and ShaQuida Kennedy.

The next generation begins with my cousin, Wesley Kennedy Jr., who was the first of my cousins or family who I ever laid eyes on while watching a high school football game. Since everyone always mistook Wesley for Westley, and my family lived on the West side of Savannah, Georgia. The nickname, West number 7, was given to him. Wesley played for Windsor Forest, which was a predominantly white school at that time. He was a very popular black male on the south side of Savannah, Georgia. This meant a different look for my family for the first time, almost promising that he would be the first to go pro in my family. Wesley was a big running back and linebacker who started both positions. Wesley also was known for putting players out of the game on both sides of the line.

He was granted the Heisman trophy in High School. Savannah State, which tried not to make the same mistake they made with my uncle Breeze, was the first to knock on his door. Even though my cousin Wesley had trouble with his schoolwork and SAT score, they were still very interested. When my father and uncles attended High School, taking the SAT was just a high school graduation requirement. This left the door open to many talented people who was not very great with test taking and schoolwork. For a full scholarship at his time of graduation from high school, I believe all you needed was a 570, but I think it was not the schoolwork that was the problem for Wesley, it was the women. Every black girl from the South Side to the West Side wanted to be with him. This was a major distraction for my cousin which clouded his judgment in making the decision to no longer continue his football career. Wesley has been from job to job since his high school graduation, but still provides for his family and the new addition of revenge is named Wesley Kennedy Jr. III.

My brother, Jamell Coast called Bo Leg and sometimes Work Horse 34, was a 209 lb and 6'2 running back coming in his freshmen year and also ran a 4.4 in the forty yard dash. His coach was my first high school coach named Chewy Slitt. This left very big shoes for me to fill, being that he was twice my size and just as fast as I was, my brother could give me a twenty yard head start within a hundred yards and catch me when I was about eleven years old. *That's fast* considering the fact I was not slow at all. My brother and I attended the same high school. The great Beach High Bulldogs which was my father and uncles' rival school back in the day. One of the greatest memories I will never forget in watching any football game for the rest of my life is when Beach High Bulldogs takes on Johnson High School Atom Smashers in a Friday night game.

My brother is in the backfield when the ball is snap, he then takes off to the left side of the line, fakes one person out as he passes the line of scrimmage. When the next defender comes, he runs them over; when the next defender comes, he runs them over; when the next defender comes, he runs them over too. By this time everyone is just watching, with the exception of one player, who jumps on his back and could have been blocked if his teammate was not watching him run, he would have scored but got tackled on the three yard line. I think that will be the greatest play I will ever witness live in person. My brother was my football hero and role model. When his graduation year came, the SAT score for a full scholarship was at 620 and he also had trouble with test taking, nevertheless, everybody wanted my brother. Nebraska wanted to red shirt my brother and sent him many letters. In one of the letters it read, "We have been following your senior year career and we are very interested in you wearing the number 1 jersey."

It was not drugs or women that made my brother decide to end his career, it was money. I think if my brother could do it all over again, he would have taken that opportunity. Nevertheless, my brother did graduate from Savannah Technical College where he received a certificate in Masonry and went to truck driving school which gained him his commercial driver's license (CDL). Now he is a truck driver who owns his own truck. He has two sons named Jamell Coast II and Jalil Coast and a daughter that is yet to be born named Jada Coast as of June 14, 2013.

Last but not least this story ends with me, Deon L. Coast (Sonic) (Sports Car number 3). Though I never made the decision to quit, I vowed to myself that I would never quit; my dream was snatched away from me. It even left an uncomfortable burden before my two nephews and son who was born Jaden Coast, that I would be the last to have a chance to reach the professional level and the first to graduate from a university, but it is a long story before I can get to that part. Now the funny thing with me is, I never got the chance to get used to one coach after leaving middle school. I went through three coaches in high school and three coaches in college, you think that's amazing? You haven't heard anything yet. But it all starts in Pop Warner were my uncle Breeze and Wesley are the head of the organization. Ready for the story of a lifetime! Let's begin with the first day of practice.

Pop Warner

When playing on the Pop Warner level, most organizations did not check for grades. My uncles were very concerned about every player and the grades they made. At times if you did not pass your classes, or a teacher reported you as having a bad progress in academics, you were suspended from a game or cut from the team. Most players who had bad grades did not like this, and they would join other organizations. If you made a C, you would get fired up, if you made an F, you would get fired up two times. I will tell you what fired up is later in the story. We were also a team who believed in putting God in everything we did, I think that this made our organization thrive and most parents flocked to our organization because of that very fact.

Before we could enter on the field, we would have to kneel down and recite the Father's Prayer. At the end of every practice, we would do the same and also recite the Psalm 23 as it follows:

> As I walk through the valley of the shadow of death; I shall fear no evil; for thou are with me; thy rod thy staff comfort me; thy prepare the table before me in the presences of thy enemy; thy anoint my head with oil; my cup runneth over; surely goodness and mercy shall follow me; all the days of my life; and I shall dwell in the house of the Lord forever.

These are powerful words I kept with me in my times of struggle. I think it's the very reason my talent always shined. Through the slander and doubt, no one could touch me. I used this prayer all the way to the last day of my career. Baseball was the first sport I had ever played, but knowing my father was a football star made it difficult for me to really enjoy. While signing up for the Liberty City Vikings, which was also the name of my neighborhood and football team, it gave me a very busy schedule because I also had piano lessons. When my piano teacher realized I was playing by ear and started making me play notes. I then quit piano lessons, it often made me late to football practice and sometimes I did not make it at all. I was too tired leaving school, going to piano lessons, and then to football practice. This made my uncles very mad, I was choosing piano lessons over football, so on my very first day of being fully equipped for full contact football, I was ambushed with a surprise. Let me remind you, I knew nothing at all about football at this point, besides there is a runner and somebody who tackles. So my very first coach of the division I was in at the time surprised me.

In 1990, my very first coach of the Pee Wee level division was named Coach Cutter. They put me in a hit drill, which I am thinking, *Okay, if I am a running back, am I supposed to I have the ball.* Though common sense should have said, *If he has the ball, I am supposed to be the defensive player, so when the whistle blows I am supposed to tackle him.* Coach Cutter blows the whistle, Dewayne Scott runs at me and we clash. He runs around me, and it is really a big deal because I am supposed to tackle him. His helmet hit me in the arm and it hurts, but I did not let anyone know, playing with pain became natural to me, but we will get to that part soon enough. This was my first encounter with playing football. I don't know why they made me play defense first, but I guess it was so it would make me tougher and I would get used to the contact.

There are a lot of stories and a lot of people I could tell you about Pop Warner football. The ones I chose to put in my book had special roles which led me to be the running back that I became in little league. My first position was defensive end in 1991, which was not bad, but I so badly wanted to run the ball like my brother and father. When being the newcomer onto an organization, there were guys who were older than me. This would be the only time I felt they were better for the position because they had more experience. Two people who had more experience than me at the time were Cory Porter, the running back with speed, and Stanley King, the running back with power. In the middle of the season, an additional player came from the Carver Height Stallions to play with us. He was also a running back named Amohed Mungin. This meant they would put Corey in quarterback and Stanley and Amohed in running back. To make this part of the story short, we won the championship by penetration with a run from Stanley King.

My first year as a running back finally came in 1992 because my speed could not be denied, but my size was in question. Nobody really knew how I could run, except the kids I played with in my neighborhood. A lot of them came to see me run my first practice as a running back. I was not worried at all because I knew I was a better offensive player than I was defensive. My uncle, Breeze, worked with me after practice every day with fundamentals. He showed me everything from a three point stand to how to always stay low the first five yards when starting out running; and just because I am the offensive player, it doesn't mean I have to be hit. I feel like it was one of the most important things he ever taught me because I was a very aggressive offensive player. He said, "If you're too busy trying to hit somebody, how are they going to hurt you?" I think this is the very reason why I never had any serious injuries, and the ones that I did have were ones I caused on myself. Even as an offensive player without me running the ball, I am trying to knock you out when the whistle blows. One important thing my uncle Wesley said and I will always remember is, "The play is not over until the whistle blows, so until then hit somebody."

I remember one day, while going over the fundamentals with my Uncle Breeze, he asked if I would like to try playing quarterback. I never understood why he would ask me that because he was also a running back, until my career came to an end years later. He asked me if I wanted to play quarterback position because, not only could I run the ball, but I would have the option to pass and control the offense. I realized the damage I could have done as a quarterback. I wish he would have explained to me, why he asked that question, to this day and now he is gone. I will never get to tell him I understood what he was trying to do.

The first people I played in the back field with in 1993 was Tyrone Devoe at quarterback and sometimes Vernest Cleveland, who also played flanker. Romaine Axon was running back number 1, I was running back number 2, and Devon Patterson was running back number 3; our coach was named Anthony at this time. As far as I can remember, Coach Anthony was by far the meanest coach I had ever played for, he had a way of making people quit. This was funny to the pure and strong, but not when going through the drills that made them quit. I remember the figure 8.

The figure 8 is a drill where it takes place at the base of the field goal. Two players lay on their backs facing the opposite direction, one on the front side of the field goal and the other on the back side of the field goal. When the whistle blows, the players are to jump up and run around the poles until you pass each other twice, completing the figure 8 pattern. After completing the pattern, two players are to hit in the middle after completion. Sounds easy enough? Well, the only problem with that is Coach Anthony would draw a line in the middle, and if you are caught on your side of the line, you get fired up. I know you are wondering what fired up is, right? Fired up is a very big and long wooden paddle wrapped in football tape. Fired up ended a lot of football careers in Pop Warner. This also made me an aggressive offensive running back.

When I got my first hand off, it was like a new me was born, I think even my uncles were a little surprised that I was so elusive. My first game as a running back was down by the river on President's street in Savannah downtown area. The field seemed so long, the first play I ever scored a touchdown on in a game was called twenty–three reverse. It felt good to finally claim my position as a running back. I knew at that moment they would never try to change my position again, no matter what coach I had or what team I played for. We went on to win the championship. That season, I scored no less than two touchdowns a game, most of the time it was three or four. I was sure that I would get my MVP trophy for the first time. For some reason, the organization was short on money that year and they passed out plaques. This was very heartbreaking to me. I had scored all those touch downs and did not get a reward for it. I was very disappointed. In Pop Warner, getting the most valuable player award is everything and I had earned it.

The next year in 1994 was my first year at the Mighty Mite level, in which Darien Thompson joined our organization as a full back, he was a big boy for his age and I would be the tail back. The coaches I played for was by far the youngest in the organization and the wildest. Their names were Coach Corey and Coach Darren, I can't remember a lot about that season but the funniest things. I remember after the games we would ride in the back of Coach Darren's red truck, and every time he would see the trash truck or people from the county jail cleaning trash when we pass by, he would throw trash out the window and scream, "Screw the City!" This was very funny to me; it always made me want to ride with them after games and practices. He would always make sure we had a cooler full of ice to throw at any bystander walking by. That season we did not win the championship, but that season I had a lot of fun.

I ran a kickoff return back every game. I remember one of my neighborhood friends, Eric Newton, played for Omar

Cobras, which was our organization's rival team. Another team that was our greatest competition was called the Caver Height Stallions. Omar Cobras were known for cheating and playing guys that were too old for the age group, but this did not stop us from beating them most of the time. I remember that season; they always tried to kick the ball away from me. The reputation of scoring kick off returns followed me all the way through high school. I remember hearing Eric on the sideline, "Don't kick it to number 3, don't kick it to number 3." No player on a football team could stand the respect I had as a kick returner, so they would try to kick it to me anyway, and I would score every time.

My first year of playing Junior Midget in 1995 and 1996, would be the last time I ever play for my uncles. For some reason, they cut the senior midget level program from the city, forcing everyone to play for middle school. We had won the Championship three years in a row, and we were looking to defend our title for the fourth time. We had an additional player added to our team, his name was Lamar Owens. Lamar took Tyrone Devoe's position at quarterback, and he had come from the Westside Wippers. I did not think Lamar was a better quarterback until we got to high school, but I don't want to get ahead of myself. We made it to the championship against the Omar Cobras undefeated. I remember this game just like the day my career ended in college—a nightmare—dreamed snatched away. I would not feel the way I feel, if we had just lost fairly, but the Omar cobras did what they do best, they cheated. It was the referee, who was an official in the game and was a part of the Omar Cobras organization, who cheated in front of everyone eyes.

The first run I had I took for granted, and I was toying with the cobras, so sure we were going to stop them. It was a hand off to the left and a rainy day in Daffin Park Recreation Complex. When I get the ball, I step in the whole just to give the audience something to talk about, then I spin out to the right and everyone screams. As I am running, I am so tickled at the crowd reaction, but I am not running full speed. This is the first play of the game. I did not realize that this game was going to be a defensive game at this point. My uncles put me in every play defensive and offensive. My friend Eric now plays for Liberty City and is the captain of our defense. As he calls the play, I feel the intensity level start to rise. I remember three of their best players: Robby Reddick (the quarterback), Jabrey Scott and Shane (the running backs). Shane runs about a ten yard touchdown. They try to kick the ball away from me, so everyone is told no matter where it goes at, I have to go and get it.

The ball is kicked to the left side and I run a pick it up. I get the ball to the Cobra's forty yard line. Everybody knows in our team when Darien starts to cry, "It's a wrap" everyone block hard as they can while giving hand offs up the middle to Darien, and they cannot take him down. We get into the

Cobra's red zone, and we know we are about to score. Darien tramples past five people on his own without any help for a touchdown. The score is now 6–6 midway through the fourth quarter. I know at this point they only have two of their best options. In Pop Warner, passes usually end up with an incomplete or intercepted.

My uncles have me playing middle linebacker. As they come to line, and this is one of the last plays before the end of the fourth quarter, I know they are getting ready to run Robby up the middle for a quarterback sneak. When the ball is snap, I am so sure he is about to run, I take off up the middle catching Robby in the back field. I hit him so hard; I lift him off his feet with my right arm and slam him on the ground. The fourth quarter ends. Its tied 6–6, the only way the game can be won is by the most yards accumulated within four downs. There is no kick off in penetration, lucky for them, so whoever wins the toss can either decide to go first or defer to go second in possession.

They win the toss and decide to defer to go second. We get a first down on our fourth play, which is not bad, but not good either. When the cobras get the ball on their fourth play, we stop them two yards short of a first down. The referee from the Omar Cobras organization calls for the chains to measure it, but before he does, in front of everybody, he picks the ball up and took one giant step, giving them a first down. One play is to decide the winner at this point of the game. In order for us to get our one play, we must allow no yards. They snap the ball and gain a yard, they won by penetration. That was the last game I ever played with the Liberty City Vikings and one painful memory to live with, but certainly not the last, maybe not the worst.

At the end of that game, we did not realize both of our teams were so good we would be combining them together and drafting from other teams in the city to create an all-star team. *Imagine that*, the city of Savannah's first ever all-star team. This was history in the making. The Omar Cobras and the Liberty City Vikings was joining forces for the first time ever in Savannah football history. I was excited, but Liberty City Vikings still had a problem. The Caver Height Stallions felt as if they were supposed to play Omar in the championship instead of us. So they organized a double header for the Liberty City Vikings, we had to play an all-star game after we play the Carver Height Stallions.

Of course we beat them again, but I am not going to lie that it was not an easy game, we only won by a touchdown. This makes it two times in a row they were beaten by the Vikings. It was clear we were in the position we were supposed to be in, and now they could rest the trash talking. When our all-star team played our first game, it was held in Savannah, Georgia and we lost. Even though we had the Omar Cobras to help us, I think it really was because we had just played a hard game that day. It was very cold and we were in a lot of pain.

The all–star games were held in Camden County Georgia, where they had just built a million dollar stadium at Camden County High School in 1996. This would be the first time Savannah appeared in these games. They put us up against a team that won the all–star games three years in a row and really did not like our presence. We almost lost until they put me in the back field, mainly this game because I was a good blocker. Robby and I went to work up the middle and scored. Then an interception by Eric Newton sewed the game up defeating the three time champions, we made it to the champion ship but did not win it, Stone Mountain Georgia defeated us in the last game.

Middle School

When I got to middle school in 1997, they were the easiest practices I ever had. Our coach was named Elton. LaMarcus Bailey, a.k.a. Sweat, was known as the speed demon at DeRenne Middle School. He was also their starting tailback and he wore the number three. After coming through little league from Liberty City, I knew that competition only made my talent shine harder, at this point in my experience of playing. Lamar Owens also played for DeRenne. I believe it was the first practice where I caught Coach Elton's attention. Barrie Sanders was one of the only players I would watch on TV. I studied my brother and Barrie's moves closely all the time. Ramon Bryant lived down the street from me and he had also tried out for DeRenne Middle School that year, he was on defense.

In a scrimmage, offense against defense, they had Ramon in middle linebacker, we had not been distributed equipment yet, so all I could do was show off my moves and speed. On one of my first carries at practice, I was handed off the ball to the left side of field. I then reverse my direction to the other side of the field and scored a touchdown without being tackled. The next play was a run straight up the middle in which I would go straight at Ramon. I used one of Barrie Sander moves just to show off my allusiveness. When getting the handoff up the middle, I ran up to Ramon, step to the right, step to the left, spin to the right, and Ramon falls flat on his face in the mud without even touching me. Now I know I had Coach Elton's attention, but he did not even get to see my aggressiveness yet. They moved LaMarcus Bailey to flanker. One other important fact that my uncles taught me is the moment you step onto the field dressed to play, you have no friends until you leave and until you leave its war. That alone made me a cold combat football machine.

So now I am the starting running back at DeRenne Middle School. I decided to go to Liberty City on the first game and it was held in my neighborhood before DeRenne Middle School season starts. I could not resist a game of pick 'em up, bust 'em up. This is a game where a football is thrown in the air and whoever catches it must run to the touchdown from everyone else. Well I was the king in this game and did not hesitate to play. While playing the game, it resulted into an ankle injury. I was really hurt; I was hurt so bad, I could not ride my bike back home. When I got back to practice, Lamar O. also returns with an ankle injury, but his dad would not let him play much that season, he was afraid Lamar would hurt himself before he gets to high school. Coach Elton was very disappointed, but still started me at tailback in the first game against Meyers Middle School where Robby R. is their quarterback. I scored the first touchdown, but Coach Elton could tell my abilities was somewhat tarnished, and by the second game he moved me to flanker. Our season started off with a perfect record 3–0. It would be the only three games we won out of six, leaving us with the average record of 3–3. Before starting high school, my ankle injury finally healed. Through the whole season I played with a lot of pain and hid it because I wanted to play. Coach Elton would be the last coach to ever show me favors and give me credit for my talent by playing the best player, which is important to know before starting the real chapters of this story. Football was always my motivation and playing it in middle school, if you did not pass your classes you would definitely be cut from the team. There was no way that was about to happen. Plus, my uncle would probably break, fired up out of storage, and pay me a visit. I loved football so much that by the time I got to eighth grade, my mother did not have to check behind me for grades. I stayed up late as I wanted to 'cause I would always have my work done. One thing she could never understand is how I could watch TV, listen to music, and still concentrate. I am still like that to this day. I just wished that I relied on my education as much as I did football. From the ages 23–29 years old and still taking college courses, I still had the support of my mother who should have been retired three years ago as of 2013. It was painful because I wanted to pay my own bills, I cannot get one female to stick by my side, even though am living good; they see this all coming to an end one day. I started to want to be respected as a man.

I had never tried drugs before; it was eighth grade summer going to ninth grade when I tried it for the first time with Michael Fowler, the brother of my brother's girlfriend. He had also played on the team at Liberty City when playing for Coach Corey and Coach Darren. I was a dedicated athlete; I ran and worked out all the time. I would go to River Street to run up cobblestone steps that went straight into the air and to the Beach; my secret to what made me so good at running kickoff returns back. Starting with the water at knee-high level, as the waves come, I would thrust my body into them until it was up to my chest. This made me a dynamite runner all around. My main work out station was exit 3 off of Lynes Parkway that puts you off on Ogeeche Road right by my neighborhood. I did not know it was exit number 3 until I came home to visit from college for the first time, for three years I had been practicing on the number 3 exit, which was my number in high school and never realized it. I was determined I would be the one to succeed professionally at playing football in my family. I was always smart because my mother, realizing my brothers and cousin's flaws, made sure I would not have the same problems they had.

I was a science genius, but hated math with a passion. At this point in time, the thought of graduating from college was not a virtue; all I wanted to do was get there and be a football star. I did not realize how important getting my education was going to be. It did not occur to me, I would not make it or another human being would use their authority and show favoritism just because they disliked me or wanted to play someone else. I always thought football was about winning and playing the best players. I knew no matter how faster, bigger, or stronger anybody was, they were not going to be better. My talent could never be denied or ignored. I never knew that favoritism or the power of authority would someday take my dream away and education was something it could not.

High School Freshmen Year

This is where all my problems start in high school, the year was 1998, as I mentioned before I had three coaches. The first was named Chewy Splitt. Chewy Splitt looked like a tall, slim, dark skinned Santa Clause with a white beard. When I came in my freshmen year, I was focused; I thought for sure football was about winning. Playing the best player qualified for the position. When I came onto the team, there were only three people faster than me. Their names were Michael and Michah who were twins and Prince Johnson the starting running back. Prince Johnson was a good running back, lazy but good. His work ethic was very lackadaisical, but by his senior year, which was my freshmen year, he had a knee injury. Our quarterback was Moon, he also had a knee injury, but an arm out of this world.

I remember the first drill Coach Splitt saw me run. The drill included one runner, a blocker, and one defender. This kind of drill was always easy to me, even if there was not a blocker. One man is not or should I say, just not going to be able to tackle me. He blows the whistle and I jump to the left and cut to the right. The look on Coach Splitt face was priceless. It was then he realized the only difference between my brother and I was size. Little did he know, I had been trained to be better, not just by myself, but by my brother also. As the season goes on, the seniors and juniors would miss practice all week, and they would have me running. I would run so good at times, they would ask me not to run hard. I scored so much at practice, the defense would have to run extra laps after practice. One day before practice. Jamie Scott came to me and said, "Man, we always have to run after practice because of you." He basically asked me not to run hard. This of course goes against everything that I was taught, I said, "I tell you what, I will make a deal with you, tell everybody on defense not to hit me and I won't run hard." The first couple of plays go by smoothly then on one play, Jamie Scott hits me hard as he could. This does not do anything, it makes me laugh, but pisses me off at the same time. Unlike most players, when I am mad, I am ten times stronger, faster, and focused. The next hand off I get, I score and also the one after that. For every time I score, this means a lap for them after practice plus push-ups.

This went on for a while, until Coach Bonds figures out that they really just cannot stop me. What really bothered me about my freshmen year is that I would be at the starting running back position all week long and when Friday nights came, I would not even get one had off. I never understood why they would reward the absent with playing time and punish the hard worker with none. It changed me in a way that I never thought I would be. That's when I started hanging out with Amos C. and Herschel Harris. They had come from Windsor Forest high school, which my cousin Wesley played for their junior and senior year.

That's when I really started to smoke marijuana; this was new to me, somewhere between losing my middle school sweet heart and being deprived of my dream, I started to rebel, but quitting never came to mind. I will be honest and say because I knew the people in front of me where not better and they were not more experienced, it made me try a little less hard. While playing junior varsity and scoring two or three touchdowns a game, coaches from other teams would often ask why I am playing on the junior varsity level. It was plain to see that my talent exceeded the level they portrayed me to be. I did not get one hand off on the varsity level my freshmen year. The more I hung out with Herschel and Amos, the more I wanted to hang out late, meeting people and being in places that I never thought I would be in.

I remember sitting on the playground in Cloverdale Park, which was right behind Tyrone Devoe's house smoking weed. We sat there for a while until a police car came dashing across the field towards us. We all jumped a ditch where the path was from which we came and from where everyone's car was parked. We got into the cars and speeded off. I felt like this was all fun, but did not realize these kinds of things were only going to get worst, the kind of profile I was creating for myself, for someone to use as an excuse of why I should not play. Being the best player just does not mean on the field but as well as off, and this type of behavior only gets worst. One day when football season was over after school. I was smoking a lot at this point in time. Another player on our team sold weed, but sometimes he would give it to us.

When we got off the bus, I had a bag and we were all coming from the store. It was Eric Newton, my first neighborhood friend Rashawn Blige and I. While we were walking down Fitzgerald street, an unmarked police car, a white Grand Prix with tinted windows, pulled up beside us. Being young and dumb we knew nothing about unmark cars, but was getting ready for our first encounter. The police jump out the car and told us to put our hands on it. I acted is if I was about to, then took off running down a street more than a hundred yards. A cop car swerves in front of me, and I get away from them, then another comes. I get away from both cop cars. The last cop car has a partner who jumps out and follows me through the woods. It is just him and I for a whole ten minutes. He is standing on one side of a park car in Mr. and Mrs. Trappio's yard while I am catching my breath and about to take off again. I am only one block away from my house with one cop on his feet trying to stop me. As I am about to take off, he pulls out his gun and points it at me and saying, "Get down."

I think he knows this is his only alternative to scare me, being I did not know much about the situation and not realizing he cannot shoot me, especially with witness watching across the street. I get down on the ground and the first thing he says, "Dang man, you play football or something." I was arrested, but before I could get in jail my Uncle Wesley and mother are already waiting. How they found out so quickly to this day I do not know. It would be the first time I was arrested. Everybody always say what they would have done, should have done, or could have done after the fact. After going through what I have been through off the field up to this point in my life, I wish I never started using drugs or tried to start a relationship at an early age. There was no benefit from them; they were distractions that led to killing my dream.

High School Sophomore Year

My sophomore year 1999 was like none other. We ended up with a coach who was in the right place at the right time. I really never understood why they would hire this man as a head coach. To me, he was a con artist. His name was Clementine Jones. Coach Jones was the most uneducated man given a chance to one of the best coaching spots in Savannah, Georgia. Although he had come from South Carolina State, to me, he knew little about being a head coach. Most of the time his uncalled for jokes and actions carried him through the season, that did not help us be a great team at all. What kind of a coach gives his football players soda to drink before and after working out.

I remember the first game against Savannah High. I actually started, but this meant nothing really, he already had it in his head that big backs ruled. My first carry and was the first play of the game, I ran a first down. As soon as I run back to the huddle he calls for me to come out of the game. This was my first play ever in Varsity. When I get to the sideline he yells at me, saying that I messed up the play and that's why he does not like me playing. Everyone is looking at him like where did the mess up take place. I swallow my pride and I wait patiently. Clearly everybody can tell that Coach Jones had a mental problem, so most of the time everything that needs to be said is said behind his back. They put me back in later on in the game and a pass play is called. When the ball is snap the referee blows the whistle while the middle linebacker rushes aggressively. I hit the linebacker so hard the crowd signs and make a noise. Tyrone which is my childhood teammate and now the quarterback for Beach High cheers me on. They call me out the game again. There is a flag on the play for an off side penalty on defense. When I get back to the sideline, he yells at me again as if I done something.

At this point my spirit is brought down and I don't return back to the game. I am trying to figure out why he is trying to run our starting middle linebacker, Fred, in full back and one of our best corner backs Omar J. in tailback. It was clear that neither one of them was better at the position than me and everyone knew it. I could beat Omar in a foot race blindfolded with my hands tied behind my back and so as Fred. I can tell we were in for a long hard season. Omar and

Fred were seniors and they both were defensive players their whole career at Beach High. Coach James and the rest of the staff treated the underclassmen like trash. So they hardly gave us the equipment and materials we needed.

One game when we were playing Jenkins High Warriors, they had me deep on kickoff return. Everybody knew if the ball comes to me it's a touchdown, no matter the circumstances. The ball is kicked to me deep on the left side. I take off towards the defenders and everyone is crowded with my blockers in front of me, as I get to a cluster of players. I did something no one else could have done when I find the opening. Not only do I jump over somebody's head, but I spin at the same time breaking me into open field with no one else to tackle me. As I land on my feet and try to take off running, I slip and fall. The only reason I slim and fall is because my football shoes spikes are worn out. The trainer already knows this because before we left the school to come to the game, I asked for some. Immediately as I hit the sideline, he runs over a start to replace them. I am very mad at this point because if he had of listen to me before leaving the school, I would have scored.

Of course, Coach James runs over and starts to yell at me, at this point in the season and being treated the way I have been treated from my freshmen year up until now. I am getting ready to lose it. Even still, I swallow my pride and I don't say anything. When halftime comes, you would have thought everything was my fault and I was the reason we were losing. He starts yelling at me again. I take off my helmet and throw it in the woods and yelled "f——k you!" at the top of my lungs. As I start out walking towards the crowd and get by the bleachers, I am so mad, tears were coming out my eyes and everyone knows why. My mom came down and we went home. I begged my mom to let me enroll in Benedict Academy, which was an all-boys school with a great athletic program where everyone gets scholarships to go to college. It was a private school and required tuition, which my mom could not afford. My Uncle Wesley and mom took me back to Beach where he gladly let me back on the team.

High School Junior Year

Finally after the season Coach James was fired, which should have been done at the beginning of the season. My third coach in year 2000 and is still Beach High School coach of today in 2013 is Ulysses Thorne. How he got that name is a mystery, but now I am a junior with no one left crazy enough to try to take my shine, or so I thought. I remember like yesterday. Of course since all the upperclassmen gave worthless efforts when they had seniority, I kind of followed in the same steps. It's spring training during the summer before school starts and I walk in the weight room.

Coach Thorne looked at me and said, "You think that cause you're the upper classmen now, you can just show up when you want and not be on time." The first thing that went through my head was, *What is his problem?*

Then he said, "You think you starting don't you. We got a running back coming from middle school that's just as good as you." I laugh finding that hard to believe since the running backs who were older than me was not better than me. He said, "You think it is funny, a guy said he seen both of you two play and he said he is better than you. I say, 'Okay then we will see.'"

His name was Jamal Bing, Smoke number 4. Jamal was a good running back, but was not faster, stronger, and definitely not better than me. Then I start to think, why was everybody always against me? Coach Thorne had no reason to feel this way about me, but the thought of me starting was not a problem at all. Though they tried to make Jamal and I enemies, we became best friends. Though this meant nothing when the first day of equipment came, *it was war*. They put Jamal and I against each other in a head on head hit drill from which I ended up on the top of him every time the whistle blew.

When they called for the first offense, they tell him to go before me. I was thinking to myself that they must think this was bothering me, I knew they were only hurting the team, so I said to myself, "Well, let me help them." Defensive players came to practice with blue jerseys on, and offensive wore gold which were our school colors. I knew this took them by surprise that I would give up my position so easily after all I went through to get to this point. I knew they would force me back soon enough because I was that good and now I am the upper classmen. I come to practice ready to knock heads off and I want let anybody run. I even told Tyrone if he runs I am going to hit him too; nobody was supposed to touch the quarterback, but I am just that mad. They tried to run Smoke and I won't let him gain a yard, and so as to everyone else. They held out a long time, until the first game arrived.

Beach High School Bulldogs took on Savannah High School Blue Jackets. This game was so big, no other game was played on this night because even students from the other schools would skip their game just to watch us play. I was angry at the beginning of this game, and I knew the crowd was about to let the coaches have it when they see I am not starting on offense. I was so mad when I come out to play defense, I won't let anybody get a long run. They ran a pass play across the middle, and I hit the receiver so hard, he fumbles and I recover the fumble also. They did trick me on one play. They saw me biting on the run so hard, they threw a half back pass, and it ended up being a touchdown for about a fifty yard pass. When smoke got his first hand off, he fumbles and it's a turn over. When Smoke got his second hand off, he fumbled again, and that's a turn over. When I got my first hand off, it's a first down. After they scored again and kick the ball deep to me on the kickoff return, I run for an eighty-five yard touchdown.

I did not have one problem starting running back for the rest of the season and playing running back for the rest of the game. We lost in the battle, but for some reason Savannah high had a player on their team who was too old to play and they forfeited their first three games. Their coach was fired, I guess cheating was an eastside Savannah method; it is where most of the players from Omar Cobras came from. The next game we played Jenkins High School Warriors, I did not play because Rodney Magwood, our center, fell on my leg in practice. Imagine that we both play offense, but he falls on me. Rodney Magwood stayed on the same street in my neighborhood. He did not play Pop Warner because he could never make the weight limit. Rodney came in ninth grade about 6'1" and weighed 340 lbs.

He was not very aggressive, but at times he would get the job done. We were lucky to have smoked to back me up at this point. On the opening kickoff, he ran for about an eighty-five yard touchdown, but we lost that game. Tarzan played for Jenks at that time, his real name was Keith, and he also played with Liberty City Vikings. He said all the defense did was practice how they were going to stop me all week long, when they got to the game, and they saw me on crutches, they said they felt like they already one. Guess who their coaches were? Charlie Smith and Coach Bonds. I ran at least three kick offs back that season, I would have probably ran back more, but they always kicked the ball away from me.

That season when we played Windsor Forest, I gained the trophy and award for running back of the week. I really felt like I did nothing special in that game, but I gladly accepted it. They held a special banquet on Hunter Army Air Field for me and it made me very happy. At Beach High School, if you are a superstar athlete, you don't have to work really hard in classes, though this handicapped most of the student athletes, and we did not see the big bad graduation test coming. I have always been a great student in class; it was just the math I hated. I really did not care for social studies either, but it did not give me any trouble like math.

That year we found out that in order to graduate from high school with your diploma, you had to pass all four areas of a graduation test. This consisted of a writing test; I was an excellent writer, math, science; my favorite, and social studies. By my junior year, I already became a district Science Fair Competition winner of second place which was a big deal. All of my Science Fair Projects placed and they would put them on display at Coastal Empire Fair. I took Mrs. Sukanek for algebra and I failed. This would be the first and last time I ever failed a class in high school and had to go to summer school. I was not happy about it at all; I was embarrassed because I love my summer time, plus I am an A or B student. Though I was a great student, I was only a great student because I loved to play football; if it were not for football, I would not have cared about school at all. I really did not have a plan to get a degree; I knew I was good at science, so when somebody would ask me what I wanted to take up in college, I would just say I wanted to be a doctor. Realistically, I knew it would never happen because I was not good with math. My message to my young audience is to be real with yourself, ask questions if you are unsure what it is you can take and if you really feel you would succeed at doing this. I did not ask questions; all I had was a dream to fall back on, and my dream was football, and I knew that I am good at it.

If it were not for my mother, there is no way I would be the person I am today. My mother never gave up on me. There were so many times she gave her hard earned money to get me out of trouble. Before going to my senior year, she somehow heard of a leadership program, and it was held in Bulloch County of Statesboro, Georgia. This program consisted of all boys and I was not interested. I must have sat there an hour, where they kept asking me to go, but because I so badly wanted to continue with my day, I agreed.

I was angry, a whole week of nothing but dudes, and somewhat school activities did not sound interesting to me. I don't know what got into me, when I got there I immediately walked off down the street doing what I wanted to do. There were two neighborhood friends who went also, Michael and Brandon. When I came back to the dorms, I immediately started to go through everybody's personal belongings and took things. It was not until after I decided to call home and ask my mother to come and get me. I only told one person about what I did while my mother was on the way; before she could get there, the police showed up and I was arrested. They gave me three years of probation for a misdemeanor offense.

When I got home and Michael had returned after the week was over, he told me Brandon was the one who told on me. I never understood why he would have done that to me, being he hardly even knew me. It created a financial burden for my mother who hired a lawyer to keep me from going to jail. This was a hard lesson, but it was certainly not the last. This goes back to saying when chasing your dreams, you must be the best person you can be, even on the down times. Living a good life is everything when you chase success.

High School Senior Year

My senior year in 2001 at Beach High School, I will always remember. If you're a senior at Beach High School, it is like you have already reached the college level. Herschel and Amos had graduated; my friend, Eric, had dropped out and his mother put him in a group home because she could not control him. I remember freshmen year in 1998, a speaker came. He told everybody to raise their hands; next, he told one half of the room to drop their hands. Then he told half of that half to drop their hands. He said by the time 2001 comes, that was how many was going to graduate and the room goes silent, but boy was he right. A couple of other people and I laughed because I knew there was no way I was going to stop playing football at that point and time. If you don't pass, you don't play, and I was definitely going to the next level. The graduation test was in full effect; remember when I said that people may show favoritism on your dream, but education was something they cannot touch. Well, Kate Marie Kennedy surely had me ready. I passed all of the sections the first time except history, in which before graduation day we would have two more times to take it, but let me get back to the football before we end that chapter.

"It is on," the Bulldogs were labeled the best team in the city at the beginning of the season with twelve returning seniors. This season starts off like no other. I did not see this coming at all. After being labeled one of the best backs in the city after the performance in 2000, nobody dares to attempt on taking my shine away. I had a new click and we hung out every day after practice. Smoke, Dinky, and Goatman, together we always did our own thing, I felt comfortable around them because they had parents who did not judge me. Tyrone and I were best friends all the way up to freshmen year, and one day his father saw me smoking a cigarette and would not let Ty come to my house anymore, but it was cool; I had friends just like me and we looked out for each other. Of course, we all smoked weed, we all hung out late, and we stayed at each other's houses anytime we wanted. They were the best friends I had in high school.

At the beginning of the season, we were in a kickoff return drill, and I just don't know how to take it easy when putting on full equipment. It is just the way I was taught. Smoke cousin, Nate B., now joins the team and I catch the ball; he runs at me with all his might and I do not break a stride either. Usually, the first couple of days of full contact, you feel most of the pain. Running Nate over my shoulder starts to hurt, but this does not slow me down a bit. I constantly hit hard for two weeks long. I remember riding after practice with the click. Every time I turn the corner or hit a bump, I grunt and grit my teeth, sometimes yell like a roaring lion.

Everybody knew I was in pain. I went back to practice the next day, full contact, hitting and running as if the pain is not there, but after that practice, one week before the biggest game of the year, it would be my last. When I took off my shoulder pads, my shoulder and collar bone on the right side has turned purple. I am forced to go to the doctor immediately. I knew at this point that if I show any signs of weakness, I can kiss the first game good bye.

Doctor Wheeler walks in and he looks at me, he said the trainer has reported I was playing in pain for two weeks. Doctor Wheeler had already seen my shoulder X-rays before entering the room. This was something he never saw before from a high school student, playing with all that pain for that long with no serious drugs. He just had to see how far I could go before he told me I could not play and informed me of how serious of an injury this was. He looked me in the eye and said, "So you think you can still play in the game this weekend." He also let me know he had been following my high school career, and he and his wife was a big fan. Then all of a sudden, really quickly, he put his hand on my shoulder and squeezed it with all his might, I flinched a little bit. I didn't make a sound or move, he said, "I got to tell you, this is the toughest thing I have ever seen from a high school student, but I cannot let you play."

I started crying immediately, calling Doctor Wheeler's name and pleading him to clear me, then he gave me the breakdown and showed me the X-ray. He then said, "You are lucky to be alive," I took a deep breath and swallowed as though with a frog in my throat. He said, "If the bone that is cracked would have broken completely, it would have punctured your lung causing death by the seconds. Though I would not call this luck, but you have to be one tough individual to have endured that pain for two weeks."

My mother and I went home. The next day I showed up to practice fully equipped to play, hoping he did not report back to coach, but as soon as coach Thorne saw me coming down the hill, he yelled out, "Boy, you try to kill yourself?

I say, "I am straight coach."

He tells me to go take off my equipment now. I missed the biggest game of the year and I took it really hard, but I felt for the next team that we had to play, which would be Jenks Jenkins. We beat Savannah High, Smoke held us down and so as the rest of the team. When we played Jenks, they did not let me start, but this was making my rage shoot up. I am hungry, emotional, and mad; something the opposing team does not want from a player like me. On my first carry I score a twenty yard touchdown; on the very next one, I scored a fifty yard touchdown. They keep me in for one more play, and I knock two people down one after the other on a blocking assignment. I am not fully recovered yet, so they take me out the rest of the game. I did not like that at all, but they knew I am going to go hard or go home.

I cannot say why we should have had a better record that year, all I know is we had every team beat at half-time by two touchdowns, with the exception of Groves and Benedict Academy, where my friend Lamar O. was the quarterback. It was then I realized how good he really was at his position, completing passes and also being able to scramble and run. Ty could run, but he was not consistent with passing, and it is what made Lamar a better quarterback. After losing to sorry Groves, which we should have not and then to Bc, we really had no competition left besides Camden County and Wayne County. Wayne County would be the last game and whoever wins out that game would go to the state play offs.

Robby and Luther, who had also played for Omar Cobras, were in the summer sessions for studying the graduation test. They now played for Johnson High School Atom Smashers. My tenth grade year, I am not going to lie; they had an awesome team. In fact Coach Jones was such a dick, I played sick and went to the game to watch. They blew us out. My junior year I decided to walk to school and smoke a blunt. When I got to school, it was on lock down. I did not think I would get in trouble for smelling like weed, so I walked on campus. The police dog tapped on my backpack, and they wanted to take me to the police station. Mrs. Nelson told them they could not, and my punishment would be suspension from one game. That game was against Johnson and they beat us. While debating in summer study sessions with Robby and Luther, they kept saying I am only one man, a pack of cigarettes falls out of my pocket and they start laughing. I was wearing gold football socks and my all gold number 3 jersey; this was so funny to them, they cracked jokes the whole time. It was funny to me to because I knew they had not really played a real game against me since they cheated in the championship. I looked at them when class was over and I said, "You two remember these gold socks because when we beat you all, there wont be anything to laugh or crack jokes about anymore."

The game comes, and I do not remember why I do not start in running back this game, but I do know when I get in, I am unstoppable. My first carry, I score about a thirty yard touchdown, and it is called back because of a holding penalty. They put me in about halt time; I think it was part of coach strategy when I get in. They give me the ball and I drive it all the way down the field, hand off after hand off, until I score. We stop them on their next possession and get the ball back.

Same thing happens, hand off after hand off, I drive it up the field and its third and short. I do not think no other school realized through the whole season when the band plays *Shake it Fast* by Mystikal, the rapper from No Limit that is a call for me to get the ball. They put me in the full back position to throw the defense off, but calls for a running play to go around the end.

They fell for it by crowding the middle with defensive players. The ball was snap and as soon as I take off around the end with no one to catch me; they blew the whistle for delay a game. Now it's fourth down and five, they call for a pass, but if anybody knew Tyrone like I do, I knew he was about to run. I don't doubt he will get it, but I would have felt more comfortable if they did not send me on a fake run to the opposite direction of the play. We snapped the ball and Ty ran for a hard first, down around the right end of the line. Guess who was one of the referees holding the chain? The meanest coach I ever had, Coach Anthony. At that moment, something must have jumped into me I turned into superman. It took me back to the season were I scored three to four touchdowns a game. They handed the ball off to me and I drove it to the red zone.

They hand it to Smoke and I knocked Luther on his butt while Smoke gained a yard. Third down, they handed it to me and I took off around the left side, faked one person out as I headed towards the cone. A defender tried to stop me, as he graves me, I spin. Now he was clinging onto my leg as I dove for the best touchdown I ever will have. I not only scored the touchdown that brought us back, but I scored the touchdown that won the game. That was the game where I earned the name Sports Car number three; it was given to me by the reporters. How is that for one man?

The next game was the best game I ever had statistically in high school. We played Brunswick High School in Brunswick, Georgia and I made player of the week. The only reason this happened was because of some conspiracy. When game day came, Rashawn B. and my jersey was missing, his nick name was Monkey Man because of his long arms. The trainer wanted me to wear thirty-one, and I did not want to so I kept looking. Then I found our jersey, out of fifty-four players on the team; Monkey Man's and my jersey were left in the dryer all melted down to a crisp. I was so shocked, I didn't know what to say; they handed Monkey Man and I replacement jerseys then I told them I was still wearing the number three tonight. Monkey man and I pulled our jerseys apart, and we get on the bus to head to Brunswick, Georgia The whole ride there I was so upset, I didn't say anything to anybody. When we came out for warm ups, I was still silent as a mouse. When coming out for the game to start, TY looks at me and a tear came out my eyes, he said to everybody the game is over because they done made him mad now. Only he knew that when I am mad, I play ten times better. I made player of the week with the most horrible jersey, scoring four touchdowns, sixteen carries, and two hundred seven yards. The road to the play offs was looking pretty good for the first time in almost ten years. When returning back to school that week after the game, I constantly asked coach if I made player of the week. He said that WTOC had not contacted the school for any awards. We argued that he had to turn in the stats because it was an out-of-town game. Finally, he tells WTOC, and they showed up with a Player of the Week paper to sign. The first thing Rick Snow said to me is the reason we had two Players of the Week is because Coach Throne did not turn in the stats from the game this past weekend. When Friday came for the TV interview, Coach Thorne said that I had to do the interview alone. I felt that even though it was my award, I wanted my whole team to celebrate with me. I immediately went to the office to make a call for all the football players to report to the front of the school for the Deon Coast WTOC televised interview. I do not think this made Coach Throne and my relationship any better.

The next game, we would play Windsor Forest for our homecoming, and it was played on the same night of Savannah State Home Coming. This meant a lot of people were in town and our game was crowded. My first hand off was a run for about a thirty yard touchdown. The next hand off was a run for about a forty-five yard touchdown. I rush for about 185 yards this game and play offs chances was only one game away. Next, we would play Wayne County for the last game of the regular season, if we win, we go to the play offs. Like most games, we start off winning, but by the end of this game, Wayne County were the victors. I don't know what got into our team, but we never played great out of town because they were keying on me, coach put me in full back and most of the game I had to block the linebacker. I was hitting them so hard, they had to keep putting someone else in that position the whole game. Ty did one thing I tried to get him to do the whole season. When the ball was snap he ran to one side of the field and I run to the other. We he got to the sideline without looking, he was to throw the ball to me. I was wide open in which I score a touchdown. Before the game ends, we put the best player out. After I run him over, the very next play Brandon B. hit him on a blindsided block, and he had to be helped out. That was the last game of my high school career.

I still had one obstacle to get past. I had not passed the graduation test yet with only two more chances before my graduation date. The next time would be right before my first out of town family reunion in Atlanta, Georgia I was very excited, we were supposed to take it early that morning, but for some reason it took hours before we actually began and I had become impatient. When I got the test, I did not take my time at all. The next time I took the test would be the last. When going on the graduation trip, I got in trouble on a grad night trip and they wanted to take my marching privileges for graduation away. Harry R. (Dinky), Carlos G., and I seemed to have brought some things that was not approved of. I had some new ports; Harry had some Black and Mild; Carlos was caught with some alcohol. The funny thing was the only thing it said on the flyer was no drugs, weapons, or alcohol. So they were going to let us stay until Mrs. Lewis found out and they sent us home. They never found the marijuana. Getting away with trouble can become a serious addiction; learning from your mistakes is a vital tool for success. If you truly learn your lesson from mistakes that you have made, you will think twice before making the same one. After all the trouble I got into, I still continued to make the same mistakes. When we got back to school, my mother went to a lawyer, Attorney Harris O., and he got all of our privileges back. It was because of my mother and my lawyer, Harry, that Carlos and I got to march in the 2001 graduation. You would have thought by now I would have learned drugs was no good for me, but that part of my life get's worst before it starts to get better. The next time I took the graduation test before graduation day, I passed. I studied as hard as I could for the SAT; all I needed was a 720 to get a full scholarship. I could not make higher than a 620.

I Went to Middle Georgia College

I entered Middle Georgia College for a chance to gain one year of college then I could transfer to a D1 school. I had a roommate named KB; he was a smart guy who had never smoked weed before. Antwan and Thurnell had come from Groves High School that was basically a Savannah, Georgia high school but different division, and we became very cool. We also hung out with a white guy named Shaun. Most of the time Shaun always had weed; where he got it from, I never really knew, but we would smoke after our last class almost every day. We invited KB to smoke with us plenty of times, but he would always decline our request. One day after class, we were going to smoke, but we heard some foot steps behind us, and we started to run. Before we could run, we realized it was KB; from that day on KB started to smoke with us. After he started smoking, he could not get up for classes. I would try to wake him up every day by playing music from Afro Man named "Because I Got High" until one day when I came back from class and he had packed up all of his stuff. I asked him where he was going; he said he could not continue school because he could not concentrate anymore. The smoking weed had got the best of him. I felt really bad, I felt like it was my fault.

Around this time was September 11, 2001 when the trade center got attacked. I thought it was a dream, when I realized it was happening in the United States, it made me realize that anything is possible at anytime. Halloween had come and because KB left, I had my own room. We were getting ready to have a lot of fun that night. We had a lot of weed and alcohol; I guess it was not enough because we sent Thurnell to the liquor store to get more. I was rolling up a blunt when a knock came to the door. Antwan thought it was Thurnell, just like I did. When he opened the door, the baseball coach walked in and I snatched the blunt off my lap with the book still sitting there. As he approached me, I threw the blunt under the bed. He asked what I threw under the bed, I said it was nothing. He said if I did not tell him and he look and see it is something that is going to make him mad, he is going to call the police. I continued to say it was nothing.

He looked under the bed and went to call the police. As he reached for my phone, his back was turned while I reached for the blunt and swallowed it. The police showed up and looked under the bed. They did not see it, so they started tearing up my room, looking outside and everywhere. Their next move was to search us. After searching me, they proceeded to search this guy from Atlanta named Chad who was in my room. When he stood up, they pushed the two beds apart where he was sitting, and a bag of weed falls and hit the floor. They took me to jail because it is my room and took him too because they knew it was his in the first place. The case was dismissed. I was put out of school before I could gain a year, killing my chances to transfer to a D1 school.

To my young audience, you must keep your eyes on the prize. If it's success you seek, then you must take successful actions, hang around people who have the same goals without taking risks. Do not let the negative influences affect the positive influenced. One mistake can change the course of your destiny, making it a very long road and causing the people who love you a lot of heart ache.

Welcome to Shaw University

After sitting out two years, a coach comes to my rescue, his name was Edwin Bailey, he never saw me play before. He said the only reason he was interested in me, was because he knew my family and the history of my blood line. I knew at that moment he was going to get more than he bargained for. I entered Shaw University in the spring of 2003. I wish I started when they had their first season in 2002, but I was ready to show out. I practice and trained very hard before spring training. Jimmy Johnson who played for the Red Skins was also my coach and Rufus was the head coach. This would be the first time I had a coach in the position to play me and I was actually his first choice. Coach Bailey was the assistant coach and offensive coordinator, I knew better than him, he had bragging rights when he selected me.

When I arrived at Shaw, I was in the best shape of my life. After getting in trouble at Middle Georgia College, I did not think I would ever have a chance to play again. I remember the first day of practice I kneeled down, said my prayer, took a lap and after I finished, I dove in the grass and rolled around. I was so grateful for this opportunity; I was in tears. Nobody on the field loved football the way I did, I would die for it. After stretching exercises, we lined up on the tracked to run. We were timed while having to run four hundred yards, one hundred yards at a time, under four minutes. I was the only one who could do it and not only could I do it, out of the four times we had to run, I did all four laps under four minutes. I knew I had everyone's attention. Of course, the other players did not like this and the trash talking starts. The next day, I was lying on my bed inside the dorm, I kept hearing, "On your march, get set, go," I thought I was dreaming. Then somebody comes on the intercom and says, "Deon Coast, Deon Coast, come down stairs with your running shoes on Deon Coast." I immediately jumped up and looked out the window; I stayed on the sixth floor. When I look out the window, some of the football players are out there racing. The fastest one on the team was out there, his name was Shawn Woodard and he played free safety. Shawn and I lined up as they called it off, "Ready, set, go." I took off so fast, it is almost as if he was standing still. At the end of the race, there were some steps in which I start to slow down, it was plain to see that I not only beat him, but I was superfast.

The next day at practice and one more day before we get full equipment, the trash talking has come to a nagging state. They do not realize, all I want to do is have a day of full contact football, but I act is if they make me nervous, so they feed it because I wont talk back. The next day in my last class, which was art, I was so ready and eager, I cannot stay still. My legs were stomping and my heart was beating fast, when our teacher dismisses class, I took off running. I was running through campus laughing; I knew they cannot tell the type of aggression I played with as a running back.

I got to the locker room door and I kicked it open really hard; I started to point at all the trash talkers telling them to hurry up. I said pointing, "I want you, I want you, I want you." It was funny how no trash is coming out now; I ask if the cat had their tongue, thinking and calling them every insult in the book. When the hit drill starts, I was the first to go; Omar, one of the best defensive players go against me first. I hit Omar head on, I spin off of him as I stiff hand him down to the ground. When the next player goes, I immediately jump back in the front of the line. After I go again and the next player goes, I immediately jumped back in the front of the line. I keep doing this until Coach Bailey screams out, "If I see Deon Coast in the front of that damn line one more time, I know something." I did not have to worry about the trash talking anymore.

When beginning my classes and selecting a major I was unsure of what to do; on my first semester I was undecided. I knew I was good at science, but this part of college was not important to me at all. I just had football on my mind, while working out late and being in shape, it never occurred to me I would need to put some of the effort towards education. I stayed undecided the whole semester. Though I passed everything, I did not make enough to gain a scholarship. After showing out in spring training, I was for sure they would give me one anyway, but that was not the case. Then the most unexpected thing happens. The side coach, DeAngelo Parks, gained the head coaching spot because he had a degree, and Coach Bailey did not and so as the rest of the coaches. Coach Rufus had gotten fired for getting the trainer pregnant. Coach Clark fired all the other coaches including Jimmy Johnson an All-Star NFL professional tight end from the staff. Coach Bailey quit and left me to the same position I had been in all my life.

I was very disappointed, but I was not really worried because I knew nobody they had or nobody they would find would be better than me. Though I was not on scholarship and was not looking to be. Fall semester, I selected Biology as my major because it was all I knew. I was determined to bring my grades up, I did not want them to think I was a dumb jock, but I did not care about a scholarship, or what I would become upon graduation; I wanted to play and I wanted to be an NFL professional. The running backs they had in front of me were named Dion Mciver and Reginald Price; of course, they were not better or more experienced than me. It showed in practice, Adam came in as freshmen in 2004 and was also a good running back; they all were, but there was no way they were better than me.

The practices proved that, after showing out in practice continuously and never missing a day, but not playing when game time comes, I started to lose hope. I had been going through the same thing I went through in high school and it was happening again. Quitting still does not cross my mind at all especially, since I have three more seasons to go. I wish I had thought about what I will do if I never get to play, what if I do not go to the professional level, it would have taken a lot of disappointment out of my life. It would have saved me from the struggles that I did not see coming and made me realize that I can still reach the level of success, such as a professional football player through a more guaranteed profession.

They finally decide to give me some play, being that I am out running every back at practice. My first had been against Fayetteville State University and they were the returning champions of three years in a row. We got a penalty that made it second down and twenty yards to first down, it was a draw. I got the ball and made it first down and they took me out the game. They gave me my own formation that game and it was called brown. When we got in the red zone and they called brown, I went in. Before we could get out the huddle, they called me out the game. They had me deep on the kickoff return team, they kick the ball to me in the end zone and I run, but they wanted me to down it. I still make it to the twenty yard line, but they are not happy about that either. As the season progresses, same actions take place, we had to play Kentucky State and I was late to the game because my alarm clock did not go off. I thought for sure they was going to tell me to go back home, but they told me to suit up anyway. I was shocked, but I knew they were not going to let me run. Instead they put me on kick off team. When I got on kick off team, a runner breaks free down the side line, I hit him so hard we slide under the bench on their side. All you can hear from the crowd was, "Damn," I can tell when running back to my sideline everyone was shocked. We beat the division 1 team as we head to the play offs.

The next game we played our rival school St. Augustine University, by this time our defense was labeled the number one defense on the eastern seaboard. It was such a big thing, reporters showed up to our practice with video cameras and the whole nine. They put me in with a second string line, a third string quarterback, and a second string full back. Putting me in against the number one defense to show off what they can do was definitely a big mistake. Every hand off

I got, I scored. They could not tackle me even once. I forgot to mention they had to run every day after practice because of me, "sounds familiar." After practice is over, the reporters rush up to me and started to interview me; the first thing they say was why they don't play you. I looked at the coaches and I said I do not know. The next day when the newspapers came out, they got me taking hand offs as what to watch for in the next game, *imagine that.* The coaches were not happy for me at all, but at least now even the reporters were aware of the discrimination against my awesome talent. It made me feel good, at least for a little while.

We won against St. Augustine University and made it to the championship against Fayetteville State. They had me in Fayetteville newspaper as what to watch for because of my twenty-yard run from our previous game during mid-season and the reputation I gained as a hitter on kick off team during the season. The game was tied at 6–6 the whole game and they were getting ready to kick a field goal. When the ball was snap, Devon Chapman blocks the field goal, and it was picked up by Torrance Nunnally for about a ninety yard touchdown. We won against the defending champs.

It felt good to be a college champion, and I was proud of my team and myself. The regular season had finally ended, and we were invited to a bowl game in Alabama. I had gotten very sick, in which a doctor ordered me to bed rest. I only missed one day of practice the whole season, the only person I told was the trainer named Roger. When I got back to practice the next week and I was running on the field, Coach Clark runs over to me screaming, and told me to clean out my locker and never come back. I knew he could not do that legally because I had a doctor's excuse. but even if I go to the president and force my way back on the team, it does not mean he had to play me. My soul was tired, I had been through this scenario for years since leaving middle school and I gave up.

I dropped out of school and jumped out of my body for at least a year. My dream was gone with no other interest in anything. I failed all my classes without withdrawing from them. I was so devastated and hurt, I turn to drugs and crime for comfort, not caring what happens to me. It was the only one thing that saved me; it was the only one thing left on this earth that I cared about. That was my mother and what she thought about me, nothing else mattered. She wanted me to finish school, at the time I returned, I passed all my classes that I dropped out on and I still was a biology major.

I was passing everything until I got to pre-calculus, in fact I still did not see destiny before me. It was not until my advisor, Doctor Dusenbury, told me about recreational therapy that I started to see the light at the end of the tunnel. They were very similar, but without the math and I would complete internship as a requirement for graduation. That meant afterwards, I could get a job and still have the chance to complete my education with purpose. It was because I relied on my talent as a football player and not seeking the real dream I ended up in school from 2003 all the way until 2013. I am not ashamed of this because if you went through what I went through to get where I am today. You will understand how grateful I am to God and my mother for never turning her back on me. After completing my internship, I graduated with a of Bachelors of Science degree in Recreational Therapy in the year of 2014.

Things I wish I had done, I wish I went to all of my coaches like a man and asked them what I am doing wrong. I wish I had told them I never wanted to be against them, and how or what can I do to be their favorite player because obviously my talent was not enough. Instead of showing out my talent and outdoing players on the field, I wish I was closer to my coaches and had personal relationships with them. I had a hard time communicating with male figures outside of my family because I was angry with my father for never being there. Last but not least, I wish I realized that my education was my best tool to success and a sure ticket to the American dream. For my readers and up and coming athletes, I hope this story will forever touch your hearts in realizing the power, the guarantees, and the importance of education.